AF556458

WORLD ASSEMBLY ON AGING

WORLD ASSEMBLY ON AGING

Editor

Dr. Digumarti Bhaskara Rao
M.Sc., M.A., M.A., M.Ed., Ph.D.

Secretary
Academy of Communication Culture
Education Science and Service
1-22-10 Srinivasa Nagar
Guntur-522006
A.P., (India)

2003

DISCOVERY PUBLISHING HOUSE
NEW DELHI-110002

First Published-2003

ISBN 81-7141-637-3

Published by

DISCOVERY PUBLISHING HOUSE
4831/24, Ansari Road, Prahlad Street,
Darya Ganj, New Delhi-110002 (India)
Phone: 3279245 • Fax: 91-11-3253475
E-mail:dphtemp@indiatimes.com

Printed at : Tarun Offset Printers, Delhi

Contents

Preface

Recognising the need to call world-wide attention to the serious problems besetting a growing portion of the populations of the world, the General Assembly of the United Nations convened a World Assembly on Aging in Vienna and its outcome is the 'Vienna International Plan of Action on Aging'.

The primary aims of the Plan of Action are to strengthen the capacities of countries to deal effectively with the aging of their populations and with the special concerns and needs of their elderly, and to promote an appropriate international response to the issues of aging through action for the establishment of the new international economic order and increased international technical cooperation, particularly, among the developing countries.

I am thankful to the Department of Public Information, United Nations for producing its full text the 'Vienna International Plan of Action on Aging', which will be of use to the people dealing with the issues of aging, planners, economists, politicians and speakers.

Bhaskara Rao

Preamble

The Countries Gathered in the World Assembly on Aging,

Aware that an increasing number of their populations is aging,

Having discussed together their concern for the aging, and in the light of this the achievement of longevity and the challenge and potential it entails,

Having determined that individually and collectively they will

(i) develop and apply at the international, regional and national levels policies designed to enhance the lives of the aging as individuals and to allow them to enjoy in mind and in body, fully and freely, their advancing years in peace, health and security; and

(ii) study the impact of aging populations on development and that of development on the aging, with a view to enabling the potential of the aging to be fully realized and to mitigating, by appropriate measures, any negative effects resulting from this impact,

1. *Do Solemnly Reaffirm* their belief that the fundamental and inalienable rights enshrined in the Universal Declaration of Human Rights apply fully and undiminishedly to the aging; and

2. *Do solemnly recognize* that quality of life is no less important than longevity, and that the aging should therefore, as far as possible, be enabled to enjoy in their own families and communities a life of fulfilment, health, security and contentment, appreciated as an integral part of society.

Foreword

1. Recognizing the need to call world-wide attention to the serious problems besetting a growing portion of the populations of the world, the General Assembly of the United Nations decided, in resolution 33/52 of 14 December 1978, to convene a World Assembly on Aging in 1982. The purpose of the World Assembly would be to provide a forum "to launch an international action programme aimed at guaranteeing economic and social security to older persons, as well as opportunities to contribute to national development". In its resolution 35/129 of 11 December 1980, the General Assembly further indicated its desire that the World Assembly "should result in societies responding more fully to the socio-economic implications of the aging of populations and to the specific needs of older persons". It was with these mandates in view that the present International Plan of Action on Aging was conceived.

2. The Plan of Action should therefore be considered an integral component of the major international, regional and national strategies and programmes formulated in response to important world problems and needs. Its primary aims are to strengthen the capacities of countries to deal effectively with the aging of their populations and with the special concerns and needs of their elderly, and to promote an appropriate international response to the issues of aging through action for the establishment of the new international economic order and increased international technical co-operation, particularly among the developing countries themselves.

3. In pursuance of these aims, specific objectives are set:

(a) to further national and international understanding of the economic, social and cultural implications for the processes of development of the aging of the population;

(b) To promote national and international understanding of the humanitarian and developmental issues related to aging;

(c) To propose and stimulate action-oriented policies and programmes aimed at guaranteeing social and economic security for the elderly, as well as providing opportunities for them to contribute to, and share in the benefits of, development;

(d) To present policy alternatives and options consistent with national values and goals and with internationally recognized principles with regard to the aging of the population and the needs of the elderly; and

(e) To encourage the development of appropriate education, training and research to respond to the aging of the world's population and to foster an international exchange of skills and knowledge in this area.

4. The Plan of Action should be considered within the framework of other international strategies and plans.

In particular, it reaffirms the principles and objectives of the Charter of the United Nations, the Universal Declaration of Human Rights [General Assembly resolution 217 A (III)], the International Covenants on Human Rights [General Assembly resolution 2200 A (XXI)] and the Declaration on Social Progress and Development [General Assembly resolution 2542 (XXIV)], the Declaration and the Programme of Action on the Establishment of a New International Economic Order [General Assembly resolution 3201 (S-VI) and 3202 (S-VI)] and the International Development Strategy for the Third United Nations Development Decade [General Assembly resolution 35/56) and also General Assembly resolutions 34/75 and 35/46, declaring the 1980s as the Second Disarmament Decade.

5. In addition, the importance of the following, adopted by the international community, must be stressed, for the question of aging and the aging of populations is directly related to the attainment of their objectives:

(a) The World Population Plan of Action;[1]

(b) The World Plan of Action for the Implementation of the Objectives of the International Women's Year;[2]

(c) The Programme of Action for the Second Half of the United Nations Decade for Women;[3]

(d) The Declaration of Alma-Ata (on primary health care);[4]

(e) Declaration of Principles of the United Nations Conference on Human Settlements (HABITAT);[5]

(f) The Action Plan for the Human Environment;[6]

(g) The Vienna Programme of Action on Science and Technology for Development;[7]

(h) The Programme of Action to Combat Racism and Racial Discrimination[8] and the Programme of Action for the second half of the same Decade;[9]

(i) The Buenos Aires Plan of Action for Promoting and Implementing Technical Co-operation among Developing Countries;[10]

(j) The International Labour Organisation (ILO) Convention No. 102 concerning minimum standards of social security;

(k) ILO Convention No. 128 and Recommendation 131 on invalidity, old-age and survivors' benefits;

(l) ILO Recommendation No. 162 concerning older workers;

(m) The Programme of Action of the World Conference on Agrarian Reform and Rural Development;[11]

(n) The World Programme resulting from International Year of Disabled Persons;[12]

(o) The Caracas Declaration adopted by the Sixth United Nations Congress on the Prevention of Crime and the Treatment of Offenders;[13]

(p) The Recommendation on the development of adult education, adopted by the General Conference of UNESCO at its nineteenth session (Nairobi, 1976);

(q) ILO Convention No. 157 concerning maintenance of social security rights, 1982.

REFERENCES

1. *Report of the United Nations World Population Conference, Bucharest, 19-30 August 1974* (United Nations Publication, Sales No. E.75.XIII.3) Chap. I.

2. *Report of the World Conference of the International Women's Year, Mexico City, 19 June-2 July 1975* (United Nations Publication, Sales No. E.76.IV.1), Chap. I.

3. *Report of the World Conference of the United Nations Decade for Women: Equality, Development and Peace, Copenhagen, 14-30 July 1980* (United Nations Publication, Sales No. E.80.IV.3 and corrigendum), Chap. I, Sect. A.

4. World Health Organization, *Health Care: Report of the International Conference on Primary Health Care, Alma-Ata, Union of Soviet Socialist Republics, 6-12 September 1978* (Geneva, 1978).

5. *Report of HABITAT: United Nations Conference on Human Settlements, Vancouver, 31 May-11 June 1976* (United Nations Publication, Sales No. E.76.IV.7 and corrigendum), Chap. I.

6. *Report of the United Nations Conference on the Human Environment, Stockholm, 5-16 June 1972* (United Nations Publication, Sales No. E.73.II.A.14 and corrigendum).

7. *Report of the United Nations Conference on Science and Technology for Development, Vienna, 20-31 August 1979* (United Nations Publication, Sales No. E.79.II.21 and Corrigendum), Chap. VII.

8. *Report of the World Conference to Combat Racism and Racial Discrimination, Geneva, 14-25 August 1978* (United Nations Publication, Sales No. E.79.XIV.2), Chap II.

9. General Assembly Resolution 34/24, annex.

10. *Report of the United Nations Conference on Technical Co-operation among Developing Countries Buenos Aires, 30 August-12 September 1978* (United Nations Publication, Sales No. E.78.II.A.11 and corrigendum), Chap. I.

11. Food and Agriculture Organization of the United Nation, *Report of the World Conference on Agrarian Reform and Rural Development, Rome, 12-20 July 1979* (WCARRD/REP), part one; transmitted to the members of the General Assembly by a note of the Secretary-General, United Nations document A/34/485.

12. See United Nations document A/36/471/Add. 1, Annex, Sect. II.

13. General Assembly Resolution 35/171, Annex.

Introduction

A. Demographic Background

6. Only in the past few decades has the attention of national societies and the world community been drawn to the social, economic, political and scientific questions raised by the phenomenon of aging on a massive scale. Previously, while individuals may have lived into advanced stages of life, their numbers and proportion in the total population were not high. The twentieth century, however, has witnessed in many regions of the world the control of perinatal and infant mortality, a decline in birth rates, improvements in nutrition, basic health care and the control of many infectious diseases. This combination of factors has resulted in an increasing number and proportion of persons surviving into the advanced stages of life.

7. In 1950, according to United Nations estimates, there were approximately 200 million persons 60 years of age and over throughout the world. By 1975, their number had increased to 350 million. United Nations projections to the year 2000 indicate that the number will increase to 590 million, and by the year 2025 to over 1,100 million; that is, an increase of 224 per cent since 1975. During this same period, the world's population as a whole is expected to increase from 4.1 billion to 8.2 billion, an increase of 102 per cent. Thus, 45 years from now the aging will constitute 13.7 per cent of the world's population.

8. It should be noted, furthermore, that in 1975 slightly over half (52 per cent) of all persons aged 60 and over lived in the developing countries. By the year 2000—owing to the differential rates of increase—over 60 per cent of all older persons are expected to live in those countries, and it is anticipated that the proportion will reach nearly three quarters (72 per cent) by 2025.

9. The increase in the numbers and proportions of the aging is accompanied by a change in the populations' age structure. A declining proportion of children in a population increases the proportion of older persons. Thus, according to the United Nations projections, the population aged less that 15 years in the developing regions is expected to decline from an average of about 41 per cent of the total population in 1975 to 33 per cent in 2000 and 26 per cent in 2025. In the same regions, the population of 60 years and over is expected to increase from 6 per cent in 1975 to 7 per cent in 2000 and to 12 per cent in 2025, thus reaching the level observed in the developed regions in the 1950s. In those latter regions, the population below the age of 15 is expected to decline from 25 per cent in 1975 to 21 per cent in 2000 and to 20 per cent in 2025; however, the group aged 60 and over is expected to increase as a proportion of the total population, from 15 per cent in 1975 to 18 per cent in 2000 and 23 per cent in 2025. It should be noted that these are averages for vast regions and that considerable variations exist between countries and at the subnational level.

10. According to model life tables, increasing life expectancy at birth could imply an increase in life expectancies at age 60 in the developed regions of approximately one year between 1975 and 2025. In the developing regions, the projected increase would be roughly 2.5 years. Men of the age of 60 could thus expect an average of over 17 years of further life in the developed regions by 2025 and of over 16 years in the developing regions. Women could expect about an additional 21 and 18 years, respectively.

11. It should be noted that, if present trends prevail, the sex ratio (that is, the number of men per 100 women) will continue to be unbalanced in the developed regions with, however, a slight improvement. For instance, this rate, which in 1975 was 74 for the 60-69 age group will be 78 in 2025, with a rise from 48 to 53 for the over-80 age group. In the developing regions, this rate will be 94 in 2025 against 96 for the 60-69 age group, and 73 against 78 for the over-80 age group, signifying a slight decline. Thus, women, in most cases, will increasingly constitute a majority of the older population. Gender-based differences in longevity may have some impact on living arrangements, income, health care and other support systems.

12. Another important consideration is the trend in urban-rural distribution. In the developed regions two thirds of the aged were in urban areas in 1975, and this proportion is expected to reach three quarters by the year 2000. In the developing regions, three quarters of the aged were to be found in rural areas. Nevertheless, the increase in the proportion of the aging in urban areas in these countries could be considerable and exceed 40 per cent by the year 2000. These changes can be influenced by migration.

B. Humanitarian and Developmental Aspects of Aging

13. The demographic trends outlined above will have significant effects on society. The achievement of sustained development requires that a proper balance be preserved between social, economic and environmental factors and changes in population growth distribution and structure. Countries should recognize and take into account their demographic trends and changes in the structure of their populations in order to optimize their development.

14. For this purpose a substantial financial effort will be needed on the part of Governments and the international institutions concerned. Actually however, the economic situation of most of the developing countries is such that they are unable to release the means and resources needed for carrying out their development policy successfully.

15. In order to enable these countries to deal with the basic needs of their population, including the elderly, it is necessary to establish a new economic order based on new international economic relations that are mutually beneficial and that will make possible a just and equitable utilization of the available wealth, resources and technology.

16. The present International Plan of Action on Aging deals both with issues affecting the aging as individuals and those relating to the aging of the population.

17. The humanitarian issues relate to the specific needs of the elderly. Although the elderly share many problems and needs with the rest of the population, certain issues reflect the specific characteristics and requirements of this group. The sub-topics examined are health and nutrition, housing and environment, the family, social welfare, income security and employment, and education.

18. The developmental issues relate to the socio-economic implications of the aging of the population, defined as an increase in the proportion of the aging in the total population. Under this heading are considered, *inter alia,* the effects of the aging of the population on production, consumption, savings, investment and—in turn—general social and economic conditions and policies, especially at times when the dependency rate of the aging is on the increase.

19. These humanitarian and developmental issues are examined with a view to the formulation of action programmes at the national, regional and international levels.

20. In some developing countries, the trend towards a gradual aging of the society has not yet become prominent and may not, therefore, attract the full attention of planners and policy makers who take account of the problems of the aged in their over-all economic and social development planning and action to satisfy the basic needs of the population as a whole. As outlined in the preceding section, however, United Nations projections show that:

(a) A marked increase in the population over the age of 60 years is expected in the future, particularly in the segment of those aged 80 years and over;

(b) In many countries, the increase in the proportion of the over-60 population is expected to become apparent over the next few decades, and

especially during the first quarter of the twenty-first century; and

(*c*) Increasingly women will constitute the majority of these elderly populations.

21. The issue of the aging of populations, with its vast implications both for over-all development at the national level and for the welfare and safety of older individuals, is therefore one which will concern *all* countries in the relatively near future; it already affects some of the more developed regions of the world.

22. The measures for the optimum utilization of the wisdom and expertise of elderly individuals will be considered.

23. The human race is characterized by a long childhood and by a long old age. Throughout history this has enabled older persons to educate the younger and pass on values to them; this role has ensured man's survival and progress. The presence of the elderly in the family home, the neighbourhood and in all forms of social life still teaches an irreplaceable lesson of humanity. Not only by his life, but indeed by his death, the older person teaches us all a lesson. Through grief the survivors come to understand that the dead do continue to participate in the human community, by the results of their labour, the works and institutions they leave behind them, and the memory of their words and deeds. This may encourage as to regard our own death with greater serenity and to grow more fully aware of the responsibilities toward future generations.

24. A longer life provides humans with an opportunity to examine their lives in retrospect, to correct some of their mistakes, to get closer to the truth and to achieve a different understanding of the sense and value of their actions. This may well be the more important contribution of older people to the human community. Especially at this time, after .the unprecedented changes that have affected human kind in their life-time, the reinterpretation of the life-stories by the aged should help us all to achieve the urgently needed reorientation of history.

2

Principles

25. The formulation and implementation of policies on aging are the sovereign right and responsibility of each State, to be carried out on the basis of its specific national needs and objectives. However, the promotion of the activities, safety and well-being of the elderly should be an essential part of an integrated and concerted development effort within the framework of the new international economic order in both the developed and the developing parts of the world. International and regional co-operation should, however, play an important role. The International Plan of Action on Aging is based on the principles set out below:

(*a*) The aim of development is to improve the well-being of the entire population on the basis of its full participation in the process of development and an equitable distribution of the benefits therefrom. The development process must enhance human dignity and ensure equity among age groups in the sharing of society's resources, rights and responsibilities. Individuals, regardless of age, sex or creed, should contribute according to their abilities and the served according to their needs. In this context, economic growth, productive employment, social justice and human solidarity are fundamental and indivisible elements of development, and so are the preservation and recognition of cultural identity;

(b) Various problems of older people can find their real solution under conditions of peace, security, a halt to the arms race and a rechannelling of resources spent for military purposes to the needs of economic and social development;

(c) The developmental and humanitarian problems of the aging can best find their solution under conditions where tyranny and oppression, colonialism, racism, discrimination based on race, sex or religion, *apartheid,* genocide, foreign aggression and occupation and other forms of foreign domination do not prevail, and where there is respect for human rights;

(d) In the context of its own traditions, structures and cultural values, each country should respond to demographic trends and the resulting changes. People of all ages should engage in creating a balance between traditional and innovative elements in the pursuit of harmonious development;

(e) The spiritual, cultural and socio-economic contributions of the aging are valuable to society and should be so recognized and promoted further. Expenditure on the aging should be considered as a lasting investment;

(f) The family, in its diverse forms and structures, is a fundamental unit of society linking the generations and should be maintained, strengthened and protected, in accordance with the traditions and customs of each country;

(g) Governments and, in particular, local authorities, non-governmental organizations, individual volunteers and voluntary organizations, including associations of the elderly, can make a particularly significant contribution to the provision of support and care for elderly people in the family and community. Governments should sustain and encourage voluntary activity of this kind;

(h) An important objective of socio-economic development is an age-integrated society, in which age discrimination and involuntary segregation are eliminated and in which solidarity and mutual support among generations are encouraged;

(i) Aging is a life-long process and should be recognized as such. Preparation of the entire population for the later stages of life should be an integral part of social policies and encompass physical, psychological, cultural, religious, spiritual, economic, health and other factors;

(j) The Plan of Action should be considered within the broader context of the world's social, economic, cultural and spiritual trends, in order to achieve a just and prosperous life for the aging, materially as well as spiritually;

(k) Aging, in addition to being a symbol of experience and wisdom, can also bring human beings closer

to personal fulfilment, according to their beliefs and aspirations;

(l) The aging should be active participants in the formulation and implementation of policies, including those especially affecting them;

(m) Governments, non-governmental organizations and all concerned have a special responsibility to the most vulnerable among the elderly, particularly the poor, of whom many are women and from rural areas;

(n) Further study on all aspects of aging is necessary.

3

Recommendations for Action

A. Goals and Policy Recommendations

26. The Plan of Action can only include proposals for broad guidelines and general principles as to the ways in which the international community, Governments, other institutions and society at large can meet the challenge of the progressive aging of societies and the needs of the elderly all over the world. More specific approaches and policies must, by their nature, be conceived of and phrased in terms of the traditions, cultural values and practices of each country or ethnic community, and programmes of action must be adapted to the priorities and material capacities of each country or community.

27. There are, nevertheless, a number of basic considerations which reflect general and fundamental human values, independent of culture, religion, race or social status: values induced by the biological fact that aging is a common and ineluctable process. The respect and care for the elderly, which has been one of the few constants in human culture everywhere, reflects a basic interplay between self-preserving and society-preserving impulses which has conditioned the survival and progress of the human race.

28. The pattern by which people are judged to have reached old age at a point set only in terms of the number of years they have completed, and where the loss of employment status may entail their being placed on the sidelines of their own society, is one of the sad paradoxes of the process of socio-economic development in some countries. The aim of that development was originally to improve the general living standards, health and well-being of the population at large, including the elderly.

29. The close historical interaction between the socio-economic and technological development of the industrialized countries from the last century onwards, and the old-age security systems that adopted as a part of the same process, should be analysed and kept in mind; however, other options corresponding more closely to the circumstances and needs of the developing countries ought also to be considered.

30. Aging is simultaneously a sign of and a result of socio-economic development, in the quantitative as well as the qualitative sense. One major example of the effects of the imbalance between the sectoral approaches taken to national and international development during the past decades is the fact that advances in medicine and public health have by far out-paced progress over the same period in production, income distribution, training, education, housing, institutional modernization and social development in general terms. The developing countries are in this sense about to age without all the sectors necessary to ensure balanced and integrated development being able to follow at the same pace and guarantee a decent living standard for the dramatically increasing numbers of elderly people foreseen for the next few generations.

1. General Policy Recommendations

31. The following summarized considerations, based on the above remarks, may provide guidelines for the consideration of policies and specific actions:

(a) The progressive aging of societies, the continuing increase of the elderly population both in absolute and in proportional terms, is neither an unexpected, unforeseeable event nor a random result of national and international development efforts. It is the first and most visible outcome of a sectorally-based approach to socio-economic development all over the world and should be accompanied by equally efficient interventions in other areas in order to ensure balanced growth and integrated development;

(b) With a long-term view to slowing down the overall aging of the community. Governments may be able to take the measures necessary to adjust or avoid imbalances between age groups, while preserving the right to life of the elderly;

(c) To this end, policies and actions should be inspired by the determination to give further qualitative content and meaning to a quantitative process in order to make sure that the generally expanding life-span of individuals the world over will be accompanied by efforts to fill these extra years with a sense of purpose and accomplishment, and that people will not be

relegated to a marginal and passive role after a certain age level;

(d) As the transition into old age is a gradual and individual process, notwithstanding the statutory retirement age limits adopted in some countries and cultures, all policies and programmes should be based on the fact that aging is a natural phase of an individual's life cycle, career and experience, and that the same needs, capacities and potentialities usually prevail over the entire life-span;

(e) As most people can expect to survive their own retirement age by a substantial number of years, the concept of "preparation for retirement" should not continue to be conceived as a last-minute adaptation but be proposed as a life-long consideration from adulthood onwards—as much to the individual for his or her future benefit, as to policy-makers, universities, schools, industrial work centres, the media and society at large. It should serve as a reminder that policies on aging and for the elderly are an important society-wide concern, and not solely a question of caring for a vulnerable minority. For this reason, this calls for a general policy of prevention;

(f) Policies to meet the challenge of a growing, healthier and more active elderly population—based on the view of the aging of society as an opportunity to be utilized—automatically benefit the individual aging person, materially and otherwise. Similarly, any effort to ameliorate the quality of life for the elderly, and to meet their diverse social and cultural needs, enhances their capacity to continue interacting with society. In

this sense, the developmental and the humanitarian aspects of the question of aging are closely intertwined;

(g) It is imperative that, when considering the question of aging, the situation of the elderly should not be considered separate from the overall socio-economic conditions prevailing in society. The elderly should be viewed as an integral part of the population. They should also be considered within the framework of population groups such as women, youth, the disabled, and migrant workers. The elderly must be considered an important and necessary element in the development process at all levels within a given society;

(h) Aging is apparent in the working-age population long before the number of a persons over 60 increases. It is essential to adapt the labour policy as a whole and technology and economic organizations to this situation;

(i) This consideration should be accompanied by recognition of the fact that for the elderly in general—and particularly for those beyond a certain higher age (the "old old")—policies have to be considered and programmes implemented in response to their specific needs and constraints. Sectoral interventions in such fields as health and nutrition. Housing, income security, and social, cultural and leisure activities are as necessary for the elderly as for other population groups, and should be provided for by each country or community according to the means available to it. It is recognized that the extent of the provision that can be made, and its timing, will be affected by prevailing economic circumstances;

(*j*) Policies and action aimed at benefiting the aging must afford opportunities for older persons to satisfy the need for personal fulfilment, which can be defined in its broader sense as satisfaction realized through the achievement of personal goals and aspirations, and the realization of potentialities. It is important that policies and programmes directed at the aging promote opportunities for self-expression in a variety of roles challenging to themselves and contributory to family and community. The principal ways in which older people find personal satisfaction are through: continued participation in the family and kinship system, voluntary services to the community, continuing growth through formal and informal learning, self-expression in arts and crafts, participation in community organizations and organizations of older people, religious activities, recreation and travel, part-time work, and participation in the political process as informed citizens.

32. A priority consideration for all countries is how to ensure that their vast humanitarian efforts in favour of the elderly do not result in the maintenance of a growing, relatively passive and disenchanted sector of the population. Policy makers and researchers, as well as the mass media and the general public, may need a radical change of perspective in order to appreciate that the problem of aging today is not just one of providing protection and care, but of the involvement and participation of the elderly and the aging. Eventually, the transition to a positive, active and developmentally oriented view of aging may well result from action by elderly people themselves, through the sheer force of their growing numbers and influence. The collective consciousness of being elderly, as a socially unifying concept, can in that way become a positive factor. Since spiritual well-being is as important as material well-being, all policies, programmes and activities should be developed to support and strengthen the spiritual well-being of the aging. Governments should guarantee the freedom of religious practices and expression.

2. The Impact of Aging on Development

33. The trend towards the successive aging of population structures in bound to be one of the main challenges to international and national planning efforts during the last decades of this century and well into the twenty-first. In addition to the general considerations outlined above on the status and predicaments of the elderly sections of societies, and the review of the needs and potentialities of the elderly, attention should be given to the vast and multifaceted impact which the aging of populations will have on the structure, functioning and further development of all societies of the world. The role of the public and private sectors in assuming responsibility for some of the functions now provided by the family in developing countries will probably have to increase under such circumstances.

34. In the first instance, it is evident that aging, both in terms of absolute numbers and in terms of the relative proportion of the elderly in any society, will necessarily change the structure and composition of the economically active population. The most basic manifestation of this phenomenon will be the gradually deteriorating ratios between the economically active and employed sectors of society and those dependent for their sustenance on the material resources provided by these sectors. Countries with established social security systems will depend on the strength of the economy to sustain the accumulated charges of income-basis and deferred retirement benefits for a growing elderly population and the costs of maintaining dependent children and of ensuring training and education for young people.

35. Changing dependency ratios—in terms of the number of old people depending for their material safety on younger, economically active and wage-earning people—are bound to influence the development of any country in the world, irrespective of its social structure, traditions or formal social security arrangements. Problems of a social nature are likely to emerge in countries and regions where the aging have traditionally benefited from the care and protection of their next of kin or the local community. Those relationships may become increasingly difficult to maintain when the number of dependent elderly increases while at the same time traditional care-providing structures, such as the extended family, are undergoing radical change in many regions of the world.

36. As mentioned above, the total dependency ratio in many countries may eventually be maintained at close to present levels, owing to the progressively decreasing number of non-employed and dependent children and youths resulting from shrinking birth rates. There remains, however, a political and psychological problem related to the perceptions of the relative urgency of covering the material and other needs of population groups not directly participating in production and public life. The costs of programmes in favour of the younger generations may be more easily acceptable in view of their value as a form of investment in the future; conversely, such costs in favour of the elderly—especially when not directly related to individual savings or wage-related benefits—are less easily accepted, particularly when they weigh heavily on already overstrained national budgets.

37. The problem of deteriorating dependency ratios, and hence of guaranteeing even minimal material security for older people with reduced capacities for earning, will be most acute in the rural areas, particularly in the less productive, subsistence farming areas of the developing countries, which already suffer from an escalating flight of the younger and more active sectors of the population towards the urban areas in search of wage-earning employment. This trend naturally leads to an even more insecure future for the older persons left behind and—in a vicious circle of further deprivation—reduces the chances of further stimulating public investment in agriculture and services which would benefit the remaining farmers.

38. To some extent this phenomenon could be considered as partially offset or at least mitigated by the transfer of sustenance funds back from the younger people who have found salaried employment in the urban and industrialized areas. In many cases, the size of the remittances indicates an effort not only to help sustain the family, but to save for future investments, productive or not. For the immediate future, this phenomenon may help to soften the effects of the rural exodus and provide a certain level of material safety for the older and inactive left behind. Nevertheless, it can hardly be seen as a long-term reliable compensation for the migration of the young, active people from the rural areas or from their own countries. Concentrated efforts aimed at improving the socio-economic conditions prevailing in rural areas are indispensable, particularly considering the migrants' return to their country of origin.

39. Rural development should be seen as key to the over-all problem of the aging in large parts of the world, as much as it is a key to balanced and integrated national progress in countries with an essentially agricultural economy. To some extent, policies to improve production and productivity in rural areas, to stimulate investment, create the necessary infrastructures, introduce appropriate technologies and provide basic services, could strengthen the generalized social security systems in force in other and more industrialized countries.

40. The slowly expanding life-span of the population even in developing areas constitutes a hidden resource for national economies which, if properly stimulated and utilized, might help to compensate for the exodus of younger people, decrease the real dependency ratios, and ensure the status of the rural elderly as active participants in national life and production, rather than as passive and vulnerable victims of development.

41. A desirable compensation for the emigration of young people to other countries would be an improvement in the continuity of social benefits in terms of contributive rights to a pension, including favourable provisions for financial transfers in whatever form the benefits are granted to migrant workers. This would be not only equitable, but also consistent with the stimulation of the development of the economy of the home country. Bilateral and multilateral social security agreements must be developed to this effect. Other measures should accompany these efforts, notably in terms of providing housing for repatriates. While aging migrants have the same needs as other elderly people, their migrant status gives rise to additional economic, social, cultural and spiritual needs. In addition, it is important to recognize the role the older migrants could play in the support of their younger counterparts.

42. In countries with fully developed social security systems linked to compulsory retirement age levels, overall aging is, and will continue to be, one of the most important structural factors affecting the composition of the labour force. This phenomenon should not be considered solely in terms of its repercussions on the elderly. Because of their sheer dimension and close interaction with other sectors and processes affecting the active labour force, retirement policies cannot be treated in an isolated manner as a separate phenomenon. For various countries the most visible relationship is that between arrangements for retirement and problems of unemployment, especially among young people about to enter the labour force.

43. Much has already been said about that relationship, and various governmental actions have been considered or taken to respond to it. Whatever the apparent wisdom of lowering retirement age levels in order to open up employment opportunities for the young, such action can hardly be seen as anything but a short-term and partial solution of one social problem through the creation of another, probably longer-lasting one. More innovative actions should be considered at both extremes of the labour force structure.

44. On the other hand, the wide varieties in personal interests and preferences among people approaching retirement age could, without too many administrative or organizational changes, be taken into account in a system of elastic retirement plans catering to the individual. Where retirement is preferred, different age levels for voluntary early retirement can be established with reduced benefits and counterbalanced by extended employment periods for those older persons whose job constitutes their main commitment, and occasionally their main reason for living. Other arrangements, such as part-time or occasional work or consultancies are already in use, especially at the higher technological and administrative levels, and could be extended to a greater part of the labour force. In order to implement this measure, provision should be made for training and retraining and the development of new skills.

45. The interrelationship between the employment and income needs of the young and the elderly raises particularly acute problems for women, whose longer life expectancy may mean an old age aggravated by economic need, isolation and with little or no prospects for paid employment.

46. Where social security systems based on accrued retirement benefits exist, the growth in the number and longevity of retired persons is now emerging as a major aspect of the husbandry of national economic resources, and is sometimes presented in terms of a gradual freezing of a large share of national wealth for so-called non-productive purposes. On the other hand, it will probably be recognized that the accumulation of retirement funds could constitute a stabilizing factor in the national economy, in the sense of providing for long-term and conservatively utilized sources of funding on a substantial scale, whose impact on other-wise fluctuating economic systems can be beneficial. In such systems, the purchasing power of the pensions paid should as far as possible be maintained.

47. Similarly, most pension payments from retirement funds represent deferred earnings by the individual retiree. The natural use of pension payments for immediate material needs rather than for long-term and insecure investments may also be a stimulating factor in societies heavily dependent on individual spending and consumption for their economic health.

48. Where formal retirement benefit systems do not yet exist, the economic implications of the aging of societies are for the time being largely negative, and will probably continue to be so, unless serious and far-reaching efforts are made to turn this liability into a potential benefit for the whole of society. Governmental initiatives to promote material development and social well-being, and international action to sustain such initiatives, could be taken jointly in an effort to prepare for the future of those approaching old age in areas where traditional structures of protection are about to dissolve.

3. Areas of Concern to Aging Individuals

49. The recognition that all aspects of aging are interrelated implies the need for a co-ordinated approach to policies and research on the subject. Considering the aging process in its totality, as well as its interaction with the social and economic situation, requires an integrated approach within the framework of overall economic and social planning. Undue emphasis on specific sectoral problems would constitute a serious obstacle to the integration of aging policies and programmes into the broader development framework. Although the recommendations in the following narrative have been divided under broad headings, it should be recognized that there is a high degree of interdependence among them.

50. Within the framework of recognizing this interdependence, particular attention could be given to co-ordinating preventive efforts in order to combat the detrimental effects of premature aging. From birth onwards, the detrimental effects of premature aging on the individual could be avoided by:

- An educational effort designed specifically to make young people aware of the changes which will occur as they grow older;
- A healthy general life-style;

- Appropriate adjustments to working hours and conditions;
- Splitting up each individual's time and responsibilities among various types of activities so that he can have several different jobs as he grows older, and achieve the best possible balance between time spent in leisure, training and work;
- Constant adaptation of the man to his work and, more important, the work to the man, and changing the type of work in accordance with the changes in each person, in family circumstances, and in technological and economic development. In this sphere, occupational medicine and permanent education should play an essential role.

51. In resolution 1981/62, the Economic and Social Council called upon the Secretary-General to elaborate a set of general guidelines for consumer protection. Furthermore, the Food and Agriculture Organization of the United Nations has adopted a Code of Ethics on International Trade in Food and the World Health Organization an International Code of Marketing of Breast Milk Substitutes to protect children's health. Elderly consumers should be protected, since the good health, safety and well-being of the elderly are the objective of the World Assembly on Aging.

(a) Health and Nutrition

52. While the rapidly increasing number of old people throughout the world represents a biological success for humanity, the living conditions of the elderly in most countries have by and large lagged behind those enjoyed by the economically active population. But health, that state of total physical, mental and social well-being, is the result of interaction between all the sectors which contribute to development.

53. Epidemiological studies suggest that successive cohorts of the elderly arriving at the same age have better levels of health, and it is expected that, as men and women live to increasingly greater ages, major disabilities will largely be compressed into a narrow age range just prior to death.

Recommendation 1

Care designed to alleviate the handicaps, re-educate remaining functions, relieve pain, maintain the lucidity, comfort and dignity of the affected and help them to re-orient their hopes and plans, particularly in the case of the elderly, are just as important as curative treatment.

Recommendation 2

The care of elderly persons should go beyond disease orientation and should involve their total well-being, taking into account the interdependence of the physical, mental, social, spiritual and environmental factors. Health care should therefore involve the health and social sectors and the family in improving the quality of life of older persons. Health efforts, in particular primary health care as a strategy, should be directed at enabling the elderly to lead independent lives in their own family and community for as long as possible instead of being excluded and cut off from all activities of society.

54. There is no doubt that, with advancing age, pathological conditions increase in frequency. Furthermore, the living conditions of the elderly make them more prone to risk factors that might have adverse effects on their health (e.g., social isolation and accidents)—factors that can be modified to a great extent. Research and practical experience have demonstrated that health maintenance in the elderly is possible and that diseases do not need to be essential components of aging.

Recommendation 3

Early diagnosis and appropriate treatment is required, as well as preventive measures, to reduce disabilities and diseases of the aging.

Recommendation 4

Particular attention should be given to providing health care to the very old, and to those who are incapacitated in their daily lives. This is particularly true when they are suffering from mental disorders or from failure to adapt to the environment; mental disorders could often be prevented or modified by means that do not require placement of the affected in institutions, such as training and supporting the family and volunteers by professional workers, promoting ambulant mental health care, welfare work, day-care and measures aimed at the prevention of social isolation.

55. Some sectors of the aging, and especially the very old, will nevertheless continue to be vulnerable. Because they may be among the least mobile, this group is particularly in need of primary care from facilities located close to their residences and/or communities. The concept of primary health care incorporates and use of existing health and social services personnel, with the assistance of community health officers trained in simple techniques of caring for the elderly.

56. Early diagnosis and treatment are of prime importance in the prevention of mental illness in older people. Special efforts need to be taken to assist older persons who have mental health problems or who are at high risk in this respect.

57. Where hospital care is needed, application of the skills of geriatric medicine enables a patient's total condition to be assessed and, through the work of a multidisciplinary team, a programme of treatment and rehabilitation to be devised, which is geared to an early return to the community and the provision there of any necessary continuing care. All patients should receive in proper time any form of intensive treatment which they require, with a view to preventing complications and functional failure leading to permanent invalidity and premature death.

Recommendation 5

Attentive care for the terminally ill, dialogue with them and support for their close relatives at the time of loss and later require special efforts which go beyond normal medical practice. Health practitioners should aspire to provide such care. The need for these special efforts must be known and understood by those providing medical care and by the families of the terminally ill and by the terminally ill themselves. Bearing these needs in mind, exchange of information about relevant experiences and practices found in a number of cultures should be encouraged.

58. A proper balance between the role of institutions and that of the family in providing health care for the elderly—based on recognition of the family and the immediate community as elements in a well-balanced system of care-is important.

59. Existing social services and health-care systems for the aging are becoming increasingly expensive. Means of halting or reversing this trend and of developing social systems together with primary health care services need to be considered, in the spirit of the Declaration of Alma-Ata.

Recommendation 6

The trend towards increased costs of social service and health-care systems should be offset through closer co-ordination between social welfare and health care services both at the national and community levels. For example, measures need to be taken to increase collaboration between personnel working in the two sectors and to provide them with interdisciplinary training. These systems should, however, be developed, taking into account the role of the family and community—which should remain the interrelated key elements in a well-balanced system of care. All this must be done without detriment to the standard of medical and social care of the elderly.

60. Those who give most direct care to the elderly are often the least trained, or have insufficient training for their purpose. To maintain the well-being and independence of the elderly through self-care, health promotion, prevention of disease and disability requires new orientation and skills, among the elderly themselves, as well as their families, and health and social welfare workers in the local communities.

Recommendation 7

(a) *The population at large should be informed in regard to dealing with the elderly who require care. The elderly themselves should be educated in self-care;*

(b) *Those who work with the elderly at home, or in institutions, should receive basic training for their tasks, with particular emphasis on participation of the elderly and their families, and collaboration between workers in health and welfare fields at various levels;*

(c) *Practitioners and students in the human care professions (e.g. medicine, nursing, social welfare etc.) should be trained in principles and skills in the relevant areas of gerontology, geriatrics, psycho-geriatrics and geriatric nursing.*

61. All too often, old age is an age of no consent. Decisions affecting aging citizens are frequently made without the participation of the citizens themselves. This applies particularly to those who are very old, frail or disabled. Such people should be served by flexible systems of care that give them a choice as to the type of amenities and the kind of care they receive.

Recommendation 8

The control of the lives of the aging should not be left solely to health, social service and other caring personnel, since aging people themselves usually know best what is needed and how it should be carried out.

Recommendation 9

Participation of the aged in the development of health care and the functioning of health services should be encouraged.

62. A fundamental principle in the care of the elderly should be to enable them to lead independent lives in the community for as long as possible.

Recommendation 10

Health and health-allied services should be developed to the fullest extent possible in the community. These services should include a broad range of ambulatory services such as: day-care centres, outpatient clinics, day hospitals, medical and nursing care and domestic services. Emergency services should be always available. Institutional care should always be appropriate to the needs of the elderly. In appropriate use of beds in health care facilities should be avoided. In particular, those not mentally ill should not be placed in mental hospitals. Health screening and counselling should be offered through geriatric clinics, neighbourhood health centres or community sites where older persons congregate. The necessary health infrastructure and specialized staff to provide thorough and complete geriatric care should be made available. In the case of institutional care, alienation through isolation of the aged from society should be avoided inter alia by further encouraging the involvement of family members and volunteers.

63. Nutritional problems, such as deficient quantity and inappropriate constituents, are encountered among the poor and under-privileged elderly in both the developed and the developing countries. Accidents are also a major risk area for the elderly. The alleviation of these problems may require a multisectoral approach.

Recommendation 11

The promotion of health, the prevention of disease and the maintaining of functional capacities among elderly persons should be actively pursued. For this purpose, an assessment of the physical, psychological and social needs of the group concerned is a prerequisite. Such an assessment would enhance the prevention of disability, early diagnosis and rehabilitation.

Recommendation 12

Adequate, appropriate and sufficient nutrition, particularly the adequate intake of protein, minerals and vitamins, is essential to the well-being of the elderly. Poor nutrition is exacerbated by poverty, isolation, maldistribution of food, and poor eating habits, including those due to dental problems. Therefore special attention should be paid to:

(a) *Improvement of the availability of sufficient foodstuffs to the elderly through appropriate schemes and encouraging the aged in rural areas to play an active role in food production;*

(b) *A fair and equitable distribution of food, wealth, resources and technology;*

(c) *Education of the public, including the elderly, in correct nutrition and eating habits, both in urban and rural areas;*

(d) *Provision of health and dental services for early detection of malnutrition and improvement of mastication;*

(e) *Studies of the nutritional status of the elderly at the community level, including steps to correct any unsatisfactory local conditions;*

(f) *Extension of research into the role of nutritional factors in the aging process to communities in developing countries.*

Recommendation 13

Efforts should be intensified to develop home care to provide high quality health and social services in the quantity necessary so that older persons are enabled to remain in their own communities and to live as independently as possible for as long as possible. Home care should not be viewed as an alternative to institutional care; rather, the two are complementary to each other and should so link into the delivery system that older persons can receive the best care appropriate to their needs at the least cost.

Special support must be given to home care services, by providing them with sufficient medical, paramedical, nursing and technical facilities of the required standard to limit the need for hospitalization.

Recommendation 14

A very important question concerns the possibilities of preventing or at least postponing the negative functional consequences of aging. Many life-style factors may have their most pronounced effects during old age when the reserve capacity usually is lower.

The health of the aging is fundamentally conditioned by their previous health and, therefore, life-long health care starting with young age is of paramount importance; this includes preventive health, nutrition, exercise, the avoidance of health-harming habits and attention to environmental factors, and his care should be continued.

Recommendation 15

The health hazards of cumulative noxious substances—including radioactive and trace elements and other pollutions—assume a greater importance as life-spans increase and should, therefore, be the subject of special attention and investigation throughout the entire life-span.

Governments should promote the safe handling of such materials in use, and move rapidly to ensure that waste materials from such use are permanently and safely removed from man's biosphere.

Recommendation 16

As avoidable accidents represent a substantial cost both in human suffering and in resources, priority should be given to measures to prevent accidents in the home, on the road, and those precipitated by treatable medical conditions or by inappropriate use of medication.

Recommendation 17

International exchange and research co-operation should be promoted in carrying out epidemiological studies of local patterns of health and diseases and their consequences together with investigating the validity of different care delivery systems, including self-care, and home care by nurses, and in particular of ways of achieving optimum programme effectiveness; also investigating the demands for various types of care and developing means of coping with them paying particular attention to comparative studies regarding the achievement of objectives and relative cost-effectiveness; and gathering data on the physical, mental and social profiles of aging individuals in various social and cultural contexts, including attention on the special problems of access to services in rural and remote areas, in order to provide a sound basis for future actions.

(b) Protection of Elderly Consumers

Recommendation 18

Governments should:

(a) Ensure that food and household products, installations and equipment conform to standards of safety that take into account the vulnerability of the aged;

(b) *Encourage the safe use of medications, household chemicals and others products by requiring manufacturers to indicate necessary warnings and instructions for use;*

(c) *Facilitate the availability of medications, hearing aids, dentures, glasses and other prosthetics to the elderly so that they can prolong their activities and independence;*

(d) *Restrain the intensive promotion and other marketing techniques primarily aimed at exploiting the meagre resources of the elderly.*

Governmental bodies should co-operate with non-governmental organizations on consumer education programmes.

The international organizations concerned are urged to promote collective efforts by their Member States to protect elderly consumers.

(c) Housing and Environment

64. Adequate living accommodation and agreeable physical surroundings are necessary for the well-being of all people, and it is generally accepted that housing has a great influence on the quality of life of any age group in any country. Suitable housing is even more important to the elderly, whose abodes are the centre of virtually all of their activities. Adaptations to the home, the provision of practical domestic aids to daily living and appropriately designed household equipment can make it easier for those elderly people whose mobility is restricted or who are otherwise disabled to continue to live in their own homes.

65. The elderly meet manifold problems in traffic and transport. Especially elderly pedestrians have to cope with objective or subjectively feld dangers that restrict and limit their mobility and participatory aspirations. The traffic circumstances should be adapted to older people instead of the other way around. Measures and facilities should include traffic education, speed limits especially in human settlements, traffic-safe environments, accommodations and means of transport, etc.

Recommendation 19

Housing for the elderly must be viewed as more than mere shelter. In addition to the physical, it has psychological and social significance, which should be taken into account. To release the aged from dependence on others, national housing policies should pursue the following goals:

(a) *Helping the aged to continue to live in their own homes as long as possible, provision being made for restoration and development and, where feasible and appropriate, the remodelling and improvement of homes and their adaptation to match the ability of the aged to get to and from them and use the facilities;*

(b) *Planning and introducing—under a housing policy that also provides for public financing and agreements with the private sector—housing for the aged of various types to suit the status and degree of self-sufficiency of the aged themselves, in accordance with local tradition and customs;*

(c) *Co-ordinating policies on housing with those concerned with community services (social health, cultural, leisure, communications) so as to secure, whenever possible, an especially favourable position for housing the aged vis-à-vis dwellings for the population at large;*

(d) *Evolve and apply special policies and measures, and make arrangements so as to allow the aged to move about and to protect them from traffic hazards;*

(e) *Such a policy should, in turn, form part of the broader policy of support for the least well-off sectors of the population.*

Recommendation 20

Urban rebuilding and development planning and law should pay special attention to the problems of the aging, assisting in securing their social integration.

Recommendation 21

National Governments should be encouraged to adopt housing policies that take into account the needs of the elderly and the socially disadvantaged. A living environment designed to support the functional capacities of this group and the socially disadvantaged should be an integral part of national guidelines for human settlement policies and action.

Recommendation 22

Special attention should be paid to environmental problems and to designing a living environment that would take into account the functional capacity of the elderly and facilitate mobility and communication through the provision of adequate means of transport.

The living environment should be designed, with support from Governments, local authorities and non-governmental organizations, so as to enable elderly people to continue to live, if they so wish, in locations that are familiar to them, where their involvement in the community may be a long standing and where they will have the opportunity to lead a rich, normal and secure life.

Recommendation 23

The growing incidence of crime in some countries against the elderly victimizes not only those directly involved, but the many older persons who become afraid to leave their homes. Efforts should be directed to law enforcement agencies and the elderly to increase their awareness of the extent and impact of crime against older persons.

Recommendation 24

Whenever possible, the aging should be involved in housing policies and programmes for the elderly population.

(d) Family

66. The family, regardless of its form or organization, is recognized as a fundamental unit of society. With increasing longevity, four-and five-generation families are becoming common throughout the world. The changes in the status of women, however, have reduced their traditional role as caretakers of older family members; it is necessary to enable the family as a whole, including its male members, to take over and share the burden of help in and by the family. Women are entering and remaining in the labour force for longer periods of time. Many who have completed their child-rearing roles become caught between the desire and need to work and earn income and the responsibility of caring for elderly parents or grandparents.

Recommendation 25

As the family is recognized as a fundamental unit of society, efforts should be made to support, protect and strengthen it in agreement with each society's system of cultural values and in responding to the needs of its aging members. Governments should promote social policies encouraging the maintenance of family solidarity among generations, with all members of the family participating. The role and contribution of the non-governmental organizations in strengthening the family as a unit should also be stressed at all levels.

Recommendation 26

Appropriate support from the wider community, available when and where it is needed, can make a crucial difference to the willingness and ability of families to continue to care for elderly relatives. Planning and provision of services should take full account of the needs of those careers.

67. There is ample evidence of the high esteem in which older people are held in developing countries. Trends towards increasing industrialization and urbanization and greater mobility of the labour force indicate, however, that the traditional concept of the role of the elderly in the family is undergoing major change. World-wide, the over-all responsibility of the family to provide the traditional care and support needs of the aging is diminishing.

Recommendation 27

Ways to ensure continuity of the vital role of the family and the dignity, status and security of the aging, taking into account all the internal and international events which might influence this status of security, are issues that deserve careful consideration and action by Governments and non-governmental organizations. Recognizing the predominance of older women, and the relatively greater numbers of windows than widowers throughout the world, particular consideration should be given to the special needs and roles of this group.

Recommendation 28

Governments are urged to adopt an age/family-integrated approach to planning and development which would recognize the special needs and characteristics of older persons and their families. Older persons should be included in the governmental and other decision-making processes in the political, social, cultural and educational areas among others, and children should be encouraged to support their parents.

Recommendation 29

Governments and non-governmental bodies should be encouraged to establish social services to support the whole family when there are elderly people at home and to implement measures especially for low-income families who wish to keep elderly people at home.

(e) Social Welfare

68. Social welfare services can be instruments of national policy and should have as their goal the maximizing of the social functioning of the aging. They should be community-based and provide a broad range of preventive, remedial and developmental services for the aging, to enable them to lead as independent a life as possible in their own home and in their community, remaining active and useful citizens.

69: In relation to elderly migrants appropriate measures should be taken to provide social welfare services in accordance with their ethnic, cultural, linguistic and other characteristics.

Recommendation 30

Social welfare services should have as their goal the creation, promotion and maintenance of active and useful roles for the elderly for as long as possible in and for the community.

70. In many countries where resources are scarce, their is a general lack of organized social welfare services, particularly in the rural areas. Although the role of governments in providing such services is paramount, the contribution of non-governmental organizations is also of great importance.

71. In traditional societies, old people have always enjoyed a privileged position based on respect, consideration, status and authority. But this is starting to be upset under the influence of modern trends and that privileged position is now being questioned. It is therefore time to policies that would avoid some to the problems concerning the elderly faced by some developed countries.

Recommendation 31

Existing formal and informal organizations should consider the particular needs of the aging and allow for them in their programmes and future planning. The important role that co-operatives can play in providing services in this area should be recognized and encouraged. Such co-operatives could also benefit from the participation of elderly people as full members or consultants. A partnership should be formed between governments and non-governmental organizations designed to ensure a comprehensive, integrated, co-ordinated and multipurpose approach to meeting the social welfare needs of the elderly.

Recommendation 32

The involvement of young people—in providing services and care and in participating in activities for and with the elderly—should be encouraged, with a view to promoting intergenerational ties. Mutual self-help among the able and active elderly should be stimulated to the extent possible, as should the assistance this group can provide to its less fortunate peers, and the involvement of the elderly in informal part-time occupations.

Recommendation 33

Governments should endeavour to reduce or eliminate fiscal or other constraints on informal and voluntary activities, and eliminate or relax regulations which hinder or discourage part-time work, mutual self-help and the use of volunteers alongside professional staff in providing social services or in institutions for the elderly.

Recommendation 34

Whenever institutionalization is necessary or inevitable for elderly persons, the utmost effort must be made to ensure a quality of institutional life corresponding to normal conditions in their communities, with full respect for their dignity, beliefs, needs, interests and privacy; States should be encouraged to define minimum standards to ensure higher quality of institutional care.

Recommendation 35

In order to facilitate mutual help among the elderly and let their voices be heard, governments and non-governmental bodies should encourage the establishment and free initiative of groups and movements of elderly persons and also give other age groups opportunities for training in, and information on, the support of the elderly.

(f) Income Security and Employment

72. Major differences exist between the developed and the developing countries—and particularly between urban, industrialized and rural, agrarian economies—with regard to the achievement of policy goals related to income security and employment. Many developed countries have achieved universal coverage through generalized social security schemes. For the developing countries, where many if not the majority of persons live at subsistence levels, income security is an issue of concern for all age groups. In several of these countries, the social security programmes launched tend to offer limited coverage; in the rural areas, where in many cases most of the population lives, there is little or no coverage. Furthermore, particular attention should be paid, in social security and social programmes, to the circumstances of the elderly women whose income is generally lower than men's and whose employment has often been broken up by maternity and family responsibilities. In the long term, policies should be directed towards providing social insurance for women in their own right.

Recommendation 36

Governments should take appropriate action to ensure to all older persons an appropriate minimum income, and should develop their economies to benefit all the population. To this end, they should:

(a) *Create or develop social security schemes based on the principle of universal coverage for older people. Where this is not feasible, other approaches should be tried, such as payment of benefits in kind, or direct assistance to families and local co-operative institutions;*

(b) *Ensure that the minimum benefits will be enough to meet the essential needs of the elderly and guarantee their independence. Whether or not social security payments are calculated taking into account previous income, efforts should be made to maintain their purchasing power. Ways should be explored to protect the savings of the elderly against the effects of inflation. In determining the age at which pensions are payable, due account should be taken of the age of retirement, changes in the national demographic structure and of the national economic capacity. At the same time, efforts should be made to achieve continuous economic growth;*

(c) *In social security systems, make it possible for women as well as men to acquire their own rights;*

(d) *Within the social security system and if necessary by other means, respond to the special needs of income security for older workers who are unemployed or those who are incapable of working;*

(e) *Other possibilities of making available supplementary retirement income and incentives to develop new means of personal savings for the elderly should be explored.*

73. Broadly related to the issues of income security are the dual issues of the right to work and the right to retire. In most areas of the world, efforts by older persons to participate in work and economic activities which will satisfy their need to contribute to the life of the community and benefit society as a whole meet with difficulties. Age discrimination is prevalent: many older workers are unable to remain in the labour force or to re-enter it because of age prejudice. In some countries this situation tends to impact women more severely. The integration of the aged into the machinery of development affects both the urban and rural population groups.

Recommendation 37

Governments should facilitate the participation of older persons in the economic life of the society. For that purpose:

(a) *Appropriate measures should be taken, in collaboration with employers' and workers, organizations, to ensure to the maximum extent possible that older workers can continue to work under satisfactory conditions and enjoy security of employment;*

(b) *Governments should eliminate discrimination in the labour market and ensure equality of treatment in professional life. Negative stereotypes about older workers exist among some employers. Governments should take steps to educate employers and employment counsellors about the capabilities of older workers, which remain quite high in most occupations. Older workers should also enjoy equal access to orientation, training and placement facilities and services;*

(c) *Measures should be taken to assist older persons to find or return to independent employment by creating new employment possibilities and facilitating training or retraining. The right of older workers to employment should be based on ability to perform the work rather than chronological age;*

(d) *Despite the significant unemployment problems facing many nations, in particular with regard to young people, the retirement age for employees should not be lowered except on a voluntary basis.*

Recommendation 38

Older workers, like all other workers, should enjoy satisfactory working conditions and environment. Where necessary, measures should be taken to prevent industrial and agricultural accidents and occupational diseases. Working conditions and the working environment, as well as the scheduling and organization of work, should take into account the characteristics of older workers.

Recommendation 39

Proper protection for workers, which permits better follow-up for people of advanced age, comes about through a better knowledge of occupational diseases. This necessarily entails training medical staff in occupational medicine.

Similarly, pre-retirement medical checks would allow the effects of occupational disease upon the individual to be detected and appropriate steps to be planned.

Recommendation 40

Governments should take or encourage measures that will ensure a smooth and gradual transition from active working life to retirement, and in addition make the age of entitlement to a pension more flexible. Such measures would include pre-retirement courses and lightening the work-load during the last years of the working life, for example by modifying the conditions of work and the working environment of the work organization and by promoting a gradual reduction of work-time.

Recommendation 41

Governments should apply internationally adopted standards concerning older workers, particularly those embodied in Recommendation 162 of the International Labour Organisation. In addition, at the international level, approaches and guidelines concerning the special needs of these workers should continue to the developed.

Recommendation 42

In the light of ILO Convention No. 157 concerning maintenance of social security rights, measures should be taken, particularly through bilateral or multilateral conventions, to guarantee to legitimate migrant workers full social coverage in the receiving country as well as maintenance of social security rights acquired, especially regarding pensions, if they return to their country of origin. Similarly, migrant workers returning to their countries should be afforded special conditions facilitating their reintegration, particularly with regard to housing.

Recommendation 43

As far as possible, groups of refugees accepted by a country should include elderly persons as well as adults and children, and efforts should be made to keep family groups intact and to ensure that appropriate housing and services are provided.

(g) Education

74. *The scientific and technological revolutions of the twentieth century have led to a knowledge and information 'explosion'. The continuing and expanding nature of these revolutions has given rise also to accelerated social change. In many of the world's societies, the elderly still serve as the transmitters of information, knowledge, tradition and spiritual values: this important tradition should not be lost.*

Recommendation 44

Educational programmes featuring the elderly as the teachers and transmitters of knowledge, culture and spiritual values should be developed.

75. In many instances, the knowledge explosion is resulting in information obsolescence, with, in turn, implications of social obsolescence. These changes suggest that the educational structures of society must be expanded to respond to the educational needs of an entire life-span. Such an approach to education would suggest the need for continuous adult education, including preparation for aging and the creative use of time. In addition, it is important that the aging, along with the other age groups, have access to basic literacy education, as well as to all education facilities available in the community.

Recommendation 45

As a basic human right, education must be made available without discrimination against the elderly. Educational policies should reflect the principle of the right to education of the aging, through the appropriate allocation of resources and in suitable eduction programmes. Care should be taken to adapt educational methods to the capacities of the elderly, so that they may participate equitably in and profit from any education provided. The need for continuing adult education at all levels should be recognized and encouraged. Consideration should be given to the idea of university education for the elderly.

76. There is also a need to educate the general public with regard to the aging process. Such education must start at an early age in order that aging should be fully understood as a natural process. The importance of the role of the mass media in this respect cannot be overstated.

Recommendation 46

A co-ordinated effort by the mass media should be undertaken to highlight the positive aspects of the aging process and of the aging themselves. This effort should cover, among other things:

(a) The present situation of the aged, in particular in rural areas of developed and developing countries, with a view to identifying and responding to their real needs;

(b) The effects of migration (both internal and international) on the relative aging of populations of rural areas, and its affects on agricultural production and living conditions in these areas;

(c) Methods to develop job opportunities for and adapt conditions of work to older workers. This would include developing or furnishing simple equipment and tools which would help those with limited physical strength to accomplish their assigned tasks;

(d) Surveys of the role of education and aging in various cultures and societies.

Recommendation 47

In accordance with the concept of life-long education promulgated by the United Nations Educational, Scientific and Cultural Organization (UNESCO), informal, community-based and recreation-oriented programmes for the aging should be promoted in order to help them develop a sense of self-reliance and community responsibility. Such programmes should enjoy the support of national Governments and international organizations.

Recommendation 48

Governments and international organizations should support programmes aimed at providing the elderly with easier physical access to cultural institutions (museums, theatres, opera houses, concert halls, cinemas etc.) in order to encourage their greater participation in leisure activities and the creative use of their time. Furthermore, cultural centres should be asked to organize for and with the elderly workshops in such fields as handicrafts, fine arts and music, where the elderly can play an active role both as audience and participants.

Recommendation 49

Governments and international organizations concerned with the problems of aging should initiate programmes aimed at educating the general public with regard to the aging process and the aging. Such activities should start from early childhood and continue through all levels of the formal school system. The role and involvement of ministries of education in this respect should be strengthened in encouraging and facilitating the inclusion of aging in curricula, as an aspect of normal development and education for the life of individuals beginning with the youngest age, so lending to greater knowledge of the subject and to possible positive change in the stereotypical attitudes to aging of present generations. Non-formal channels and the mass media should also be used to develop such programmes. The mass media should also be used as a means of promoting the participation of the aged in social, cultural and educational activities within the community; conversely, the aged or their representatives should be involved in formulating and designing these activities.

Recommendation 50

Where stereotypes of the aging person exist, efforts by the media, educational institutions, Governments, non-governmental organizations and the aging themselves should be devoted to overcoming the stereotyping of older persons as always manifesting physical and psychological disabilities, incapable of functioning independently and having neither role nor status in society. These efforts are necessary for achieving an age-integrated society.

Recommendation 51

Comprehensive information on all aspects of their lives should be made available to the aging in a clear and understandable form.

B. Promotion Policies and Programmes

77. The full realization of the Plan of Action depends on the implementation of all international documents, strategies and plans, mentioned in paragraphs 4 and 5. In promoting policies and programmes within the framework of the Plan of Action, the Centre for Social Development and Humanitarian Affairs, the United Nations Fund for Population Activities, the United Nations Development Programme, the Department of Technical Co-operation for Development and the regional commissions as well as the specialized agencies, institutions and other inter-governmental and non-governmental organizations are urged to give maximum assistance to all countries at their request. Full use should also be made of opportunities existing for technical co-operation between developed and developing countries in the field of aging.

1. Data Collection and Analysis

78. Data concerning the older sector of the population—collected through censuses, surveys or vital statistics systems—are essential for the formulation, application and evaluation of policies and programmes for the elderly and for ensuring their integration in the development process.

79. Governments and organizations that are in a position to do so should develop an information base which would be more specific than the 'sixty-and-over' one now in use and which would be of help in planning the development of and solving problems concerning the elderly. The base could cover social, age, functional and economic classifications, among others.

80. Household sample and other surveys and other sources of demographic and related socio-economic statistics provide important data for use in formulating and implementing policies and programmes for the elderly.

81. All countries that so request should be provided with the technical assistance needed to develop or improve data bases relating to their elderly and the services and institutions that concern them. The assistance should cover training and research in methodologies for collecting, processing and analysing data.

Recommendation 52

Data concerning the aging could be developed along the line of a codification system which will give national Governments information tabulated by sex, age income levels, living arrangements, health status and degree of self care, among others. Such data could be collected through the census, micro or pilot census or representative surveys. Governments are urged to allocate resources for that purpose.

Recommendation 53

Governments and institutions concerned should establish or improve existing information exchange facilities, such as data banks in the field of aging.

2. Training and Education

82. The dramatic increase in the number and proportion of older adults calls for a significant increase in training. A dual approach is needed: an international programme for training concomitant with national and regional training programmes that are particularly relevant to conditions in the countries and regions concerned. The needs of the elderly, as well as the implications of the aging of the population for development, need to be taken into account in developing education and training policies and programmes for all ages, especially the younger generation.

Recommendation 54

Education and training programmes should be interdisciplinary in nature, as aging and the aging of the population is a multidisciplinary issue. Education and training in the various aspects of aging and the aging of the population should not be restricted to high levels of specialization, but should be made available at all levels. Efforts should be made to regulate the training skills and educational requirements for different functions in the field of aging.

83. The exchange of skills, knowledge and experience among countries with similar or comparable structures and composition, or having historical, cultural, linguistic or other links, with respect to their aging population would be a particularly fertile form of international co-operation. Besides the transfer of specific skills and technologies, the exchange of experience regarding the wide array of practices relating to aging could also constitute an area for technical co-operation among developing countries. In regions which include both developed and developing countries side by side, the rich opportunities for mutual learning and co-operation in training and research should be vigorously explored.

Recommendation 55

Inter-governmental and non-governmental organizations should take the necessary measures to develop trained personnel in the field of aging, and should strengthen their efforts to disseminate information on aging, and particularly to the aging themselves.

Recommendation 56

Retirees' and elderly people's organizations should be involved in planning and carrying out such exchanges of information.

Recommendation 57

The implementation of several recommendations will require trained personnel in the field of aging. Practical training centres should be promoted and encouraged, where appropriate facilities already exist, to train such personnel, especially from developing countries, who would in their turn train others. These centres would also provide updating and refresher courses and act as a practical bridge between and among developed and developing regions; they would be linked with appropriate United Nations agencies and facilities.

Recommendation 58

At national, regional and international levels, extra attention should be given to research and study undertaken in support of integrating the problems of aging in planning and policy formulation and management.

Recommendation 59

Training in all aspects of gerontology and geriatrics should be encouraged and given due prominence at all levels in all educational programmes. Governments and competent authorities are called upon to encourage new or existing institutions to pay special attention to appropriate training in gerontology and geriatrics.

3. Research

84. The Plan of Action gives high priority to research related to development and humanitarian aspects of aging. Research activities are instrumental in formulating, evaluating and implementing policies and programmes; (a) as to the implications of the aging of the population for development and (b) as to the needs of the aging. Research into the social, economic and health aspects of aging should be encouraged to achieve efficient uses of resources, improvement in social and health measures, including the prevention of functional decline, age-related disabilities, illness and poverty, and co-ordination of the services involved in the care of the aging.

85. The knowledge obtained by research provides scientific backing for a sounder basis for effective societal planning as well as for improving the well-being of the elderly. Further research is required, e.g. (a) to narrow the wide gaps in knowledge about aging and about the particular needs of aging, and (b) to enable resources provided for the aging to be used more effectively. There should be emphasis on the continuum of research for the discovery of new knowledge to its vigorous and more rapid application and transfer of technological knowledge with due consideration of cultural and social diversity.

Recommendation 60

Research should be conducted into the developmental and humanitarian aspects of aging at local, national, regional and global levels. Research should be encouraged particularly in the biological, mental and social fields. Issues of basic and applied research of universal interest to all societies include:

(a) *The role of genetic and environmental factors;*

(b) *The impact of biological, medical, cultural, societal and behavioural factors on aging;*

(c) *The influence of economic and demographic factors (including migration) on societal planning;*

(d) *The use of skills, expertise, knowledge and cultural potential of the aging;*

(e) *The postponement of negative functional consequences of aging;*

(f) *Health and social services for the aging as well as studies of co-ordinated programmes;*

(g) *Training and education.*

Such research should be generally planned and carried out by researchers closely acquainted with national and regional conditions, being granted the independence necessary for innovation and diffusion. States, intergovernmental organizations and non-governmental organizations should carry out more research and studies on the developmental and humanitarian aspects of aging, co-operate in this field and exchange their findings in order to provide a logical basis for policies related to aging in general.

Recommendation 61

States, inter-governmental organizations and non-governmental organizations should encourage the establishment of institutions specializing in the teaching of gerontology, geriatrics and geriatric psychology in countries where such institutions do not exist.

Recommendation 62

International exchange and research co-operation as well as data collection should be promoted in all fields having a bearing on aging, in order to provide a rational basis for future social policies and action. Special emphasis should be placed on comparative and cross-cultural studies on aging. Inter-disciplinary approaches be stressed.

Recommendations for Implementation

A. Role of Governments

86. The success of this Plan of Action will depend largely on action undertaken by Governments to create conditions and broad possibilities for full participation of the citizens, particularly the elderly. To this end, Governments are urged to devote more attention to the question of aging and to utilize fully the support provided by intergovernmental and non-governmental organizations, including retirees' and elderly people's organizations.

87. Since wide divergencies exist with respect to the situation of the aging in various societies, cultures and regions—as reflected in different needs and problems—each country should decide upon its own national strategy and identify its own targets and priorities within the Plan. A clear commitment should be made at all levels of

Government to take appropriate action to achieve those targets and give effect to those priorities.

88. Governments can play an important role with regard to the Plan of Action by evaluating and assessing the aging process from the individual and demographic points of view, in order to determine the implications for development of these processes in the light of the prevailing political, social, cultural, religious and economic situation.

89. The architects of national policies and strategies for the implementation of the Plan of Action should recognize that the aging are not a homogeneous group and be sensitive to the wide differences and needs of the aging at various stages of their lives. Governments should pay special attention to improving the lot of elderly women, who are often at a severe disadvantage.

90. The establishment of inter-disciplinary and multisectoral machinery within Governments can be an effective means of ensuring that the question of the aging of the population is taken into account in national development planning, that the needs of the elderly are given the attention they merit, and that the elderly are fully integrated into society.

91. These action will gain in effectiveness if their preparation, implementation and follow-up are well co-ordinated at various geopolitical levels. The co-ordination must flow from co-operation between those in positions of responsibility in all sectors and the representatives of pensioners and the aged, in order to ensure the participation of the latter when decisions of direct concern to them are being taken. Hence, it would be appropriate to consider the setting up of corresponding planning, programming and co-ordinating bodies at the national level.

92. In certain countries, some of the objectives of the Plan of Action have already been achieved; in others they may only be accomplished progressively. Moreover, by their very nature, some measures will take longer to implement than others. Governments are urged, therefore, to establish short-, medium-and long-term objectives with a view to facilitating implementation of the Plan, in the light of their resources and priorities.

93. Governments should, if necessary, retain in a suitable form (or encourage the formation of) the mechanisms established at the national level to prepare for the World Assembly on Aging, in order to be ready to facilitate the planning, implementation and evaluation of the activities recommended by the World Assembly.

B. Role of International and Regional Co-operation

1. Global Action

94. International co-operation in the implementation of the programme of action on the establishment *inter alia* of a new international economic order and of the International Development Strategy for the Third United Nations Development Decade, based on the peaceful coexistence of States having different social systems, is essential to achieving the goals of the Plan of Action and can take the form of bilateral and multilateral co-operation between Governments and by utilizing the United Nations system. Such co-operation could take the form of direct assistance (technical or financial), in response to national or regional requests, co-operative research, or the exchange of information and experience.

95. The General Assembly, the Economic and Social Council and all its Appropriate subsidiary bodies, in particular the Commission for Social Development, the Governing Council of the United Nations Development Programme, and the legislative and policy-making bodies of the concerned specialized agencies and inter-governmental organizations are urged to give careful consideration to the Plan of Action and to ensure an appropriate response to it.

96. In view of the role that the Centre for Social Development and Humanitarian Affairs of the Department of International Economic and Social Affairs has been playing within the United Nations system in matters related to the aging, it should be strengthened in order to continue to serve as the focal point for activities in that respect; to this end the Secretary-General of the United Nations is requested, within the existing global resources of the United Nations, to give due consideration to the provision of appropriate increased resources for the implementation of the Plan of Action, which will be primarily at the national level.

97. The Administrative Committee on Co-ordination should consider the implications of the Plan of Action for the United Nations systems with a view to continued liaison and co-ordination in implementing the provisions of the Plan.

98. The need to develop new guidelines in areas of concern to the elderly should be kept constantly under review in relation to the implementation of the Plan.

99. Governments, national and local non-governmental voluntary organizations and international non-governmental organizations are urged to join in the co-operative effort to accomplish the objectives of the Plan. They should strengthen their activities by encouraging the formation of and utilizing regular channels of communication at the national level for consulting with the elderly on policies and programmes that affect their lives. Governments are also urged to encourage and, where possible, support national and private organizations dealing with matters concerning the elderly and the aging of the population.

100. All States are invited to consider designating a national 'Day for the Aging' in conformity with General Assembly resolution 36/20 of 9 November 1981.

101. The International Plan of Action on Aging should be brought to the attention of the appropriate United Nations bodies responsible for preparations for the International Conference on Population (1984), so that its conclusions and recommendations could be taken into account in preparing the proposals for the further implementation of the World Population Plan of Action.

(a) Technical Co-operation

102. The United Nations, and in particular the United Nations Development Programme and the Department of Technical Co-operation for Development, together with the specialized agencies, should carry out technical co-operation activities in support of the objectives of the Plan of Action. The Centre for Social Development and Humanitarian Affairs should continue to promote, and provide substantive support to, all such activities.

103. The voluntary Trust Fund for the World Assembly on Aging, established by General Assembly resolution 35/129, should be used, as requested by the General Assembly, to meet the rapidly increasing needs of the aging in the developing countries, in particular in the least developed ones. The payment of voluntary public and private contributions should be encouraged. The Trust Fund should be administered by the Centre for Social Development and Humanitarian Affairs.

104. Furthermore, as requested by the General Assembly in its resolution 36/20, the Fund should be used to encourage greater interest in the developing countries in matters related to aging and to assist the Governments of these countries, at their request, in formulating and implementing policies and programmes for the elderly. It should also be used for technical co-operation and research related to the aging of populations and for promoting co-operation among developing countries in the exchange of the relevant information and technology.

105. Aging is a population issue which affects development and which requires increasing international assistance and co-operation and, therefore, the United Nations Fund for Population Activities urged, in co-operation with all organizations responsible for international population assistance, to continue and to strengthen its assistance in that field, particularly in developing countries.

(b) Exchange of Information and Experience

106. The exchange of information and experience at the international level is an effective means of stimulating progress and encouraging the adoption of measures to respond to the economic and social implications of the aging of the population, and to meet the needs of older persons. Countries with different political, economic and social systems and cultures and at different stages of development have benefited from the common knowledge of problems, difficulties and achievements and from solutions worked out jointly.

107. Meetings and seminars have proved to be most valuable in providing a regional and international exchange of information and experience and should be continued. These could focus, *inter alia,* on promoting technical co-operation among developing countries and on monitoring the implementation of the Plan of Action.

108. The Centre for Social Development and Humanitarian Affairs should co-ordinate the activities of regional and subregional research and development centres in the United Nations system, promote the preparation of information materials, as well as the constant exchange of information on problems and policies related to aging and the training of personnel, and facilitate activities related to technical co-operation among developing countries in collaboration with concerned Governments and regions.

109. With respect to the exchange of information about matters concerning aging, it is essential that standardized definitions, terms and research methodologies be developed; the United Nations should treat these matters with all due importance.

110. The United Nations bodies concerned should encourage Governments and the international community to pay special attention to developing programmes, projects an activities that will give older persons the skills, training and opportunities necessary to improve their situation and enable them to participate fully and effectively in the total development effort. Special attention should be given to training courses in technologies that will enable older persons to continue to work in agriculture.

111. The International Plan of Action on Aging should be transmitted to the unit in the United Nations Secretariat responsible for International Youth Year (1985) in order that that unit may bring the recommendations and conclusion of the World Assembly on Aging—particularly as they relate to inter-generational matters—to the attention of national planning committees concerned with developing ideas for the Youth Year.

(c) Formulation and Implementation of International Guidelines

112. The appropriate organizations should undertake studies on and review periodically the effectiveness of existing international guidelines and instruments related to the subject of aging, in order to determine their adequacy in the light of changing conditions in the modern world and the experience gained since their adoption.

2. Regional Action

113. Effective implementation of the Plan will also require action at the regional level. All institutions having regional mandates are therefore called upon to review the objectives of the Plan and contribute to their implementation. In this respect, a central role should be played by the United Nations regional commissions.

114. In order to carry out the above-mentioned functions, Governments members of regional commissions should take steps to ensure that their regular programme of activities take into account the problems of aging.

115. Furthermore, in co-ordination with the conduct of the international review discussed above, the regional commission should organize the periodic review of regional plans.

C. Assessment, Review and Appraisal

116. It is essential that assessment, evaluation and review should take place at the national level, at intervals to be determined by each country.

117. Regional appraisal and review should focus on the special role regional action can play and the particular advantages it can offer in such fields as training, research and technical co-operation among developing countries.

118. It is recommended that the Commission for Social Development should be designated the intergovernmental body to review the implementation of the Plan of Action every four years and to make proposals for updating the Plan as considered necessary. The findings of this exercise should be transmitted through the Economic and Social Council to the General Assembly for consideration. To assist the Commission in its work it should be provided with periodic reports on progress made within the United Nations system in achieving the goals and objectives of the Plan. The Centre for Social Development and Humanitarian Affairs should serve as the co-ordinator of this process.

Annex

States that Represented at the World Assembly on Aging

Afganistan
Algeria
Angola
Argentina
Australia
Austria
Bahrain
Bangladesh
Belgium
Benin
Botswana
Brazil
Bulgaria
Burundi
Byelorussian Soviet Socialist Republic
Canada
Cape Verde
Central African Republic
Chad
Chile
China
Colombia
Congo
Costa Rica
Cuba
Cyprus
Czechoslovakia
Democratic Kampuchea
Democratic Yemen
Denmark
Djibouti
Dominican Republic

Ecuador	Kenya
Egypt	Kuwait
El Salvador	Lebanon
Ethiopia	Lesotho
Finland	Liberia
France	Libyan Arab Jamahiriya
Gabon	Luxembourg
Gambia	Malawi
German Democratic Republic	Malaysia
Germany, Federal Republic of	Maldives
Greece	Mali
Guatemala	Malta
Guinea	Mauritius
Guinea-Bissau	Mexico
Haiti	Morocco
Holy See	Mozambique
Hungary	Netherlands
Iceland	New Zealand
India	Nicaragua
Indonesia	Niger
Iran	Nigeria
Iraq	Norway
Ireland	Pakistan
Israel	Panama
Italy	Peru
Ivory Coast	Philippines
Jamaica	Poland
Japan	Portugal
Jordan	

Republic of Korea
Romania
Rawanda
San Marino
Saudi Arabia
Senegal
Seychelles
Spain
Sri Lanka
Sudan
Suriname
Swaziland
Sweden
Switzerland
Syrian Arab Republic
Thailand
Togo
Trinidad and Tobago
Tunisia
Turkey
Ukrainian Soviet Socialist Republic
Union of Soviet Socialist Republics
United Arab Emirates
United Kingdom of Great Britain and Northern Ireland
United Republic of Cameroon
United Republic of Tanzania
United States of America
Upper Volta
Uruguay
Venezuela
Viet Nam
Yeman
Yogoslavia
Zaire
Zambia

The United Nations Council for Namibia was represented at the Assembly.